I HEARD YOU, LORD

ERLINE DENNIS

authorHOUSE

AuthorHouse™
1663 Liberty Drive
Bloomington, IN 47403
www.authorhouse.com
Phone: 833-262-8899

Published by AuthorHouse 08/31/2023

ISBN: 979-8-8230-1388-8 (sc)
ISBN: 979-8-8230-1387-1 (e)

Library of Congress Control Number: 2023916433

Print information available on the last page.

In memory of my dear Mother

who is so deeply missed. The pain is
still so great. You are truly missed
by all who knew you. If only you knew!
But when I think about it, I GUESS YOU DO.
We know you are looking down at us from above.
And doing the Lord's will with such great love.

And to you, Patricia

my sister and closest and dearest friend,
who came into my life in-my darkest hours,
who has given so much of herself and shared
her love of the Lord with me. She continues
to walk day by day with me. God bless you, Pat.
And may you continue to let the Lord's light shine.

And also,

to my pride and joy, Shanté Reneé

CONTENTS

I HEARD YOU, LORD

I heard you, Lord, when you spoke to me.
Even though I was not down on bended knee.

I heard you, Lord, when you said to me,
I am here, not far from thee.

I heard you, Lord, when you said take my hand,
I will walk with you throughout this land.

I heard you, Lord, say come walk with me.
For I will show you many, many things,
You need to see.

I heard your voice when you spoke to my heart,
And said,
"Now, my child, it is THE TIME, to do your part."

Speak from the heart and people will hear
Everything you say
And understand the words ever so clear.

Tell them what you feel,
And what you know.
And how the Lord's love continues to grow.

But most important of all, Lord, I heard you say,
I am with you today, tomorrow and ALWAYS.

WHEN THE STORMS COME

Why are there so many showers in life?
They may start out as drizzles
And then they start to brew
And can turn into an ugly sight.

A lot of times these showers do turn
Into grave and bleak thunderstorms,
Leaving your spirit upside down
And so fragile and torn.

There is always a little drizzle of rain somewhere.
But then there are times when the skies do clear,
Letting you steer a course without trials to face,
For this is truly the Lord's ever-loving grace.

When you think you have weathered the storm
And you feel peace and joy within,
Then something else comes along
And snatches the joy away,
Leaving you scattered, bound and torn,
And in utter disarray.

How quickly the peace and joy
Become lost and hard to find.
As you look at all the confusion and chaos
That is left behind.

I am often reminded to remain strong
Because our Lord has the remedy
To right any wrong.

And to hold onto the joy
That I feel inside,
Letting no man or thing steal
And try to defy.

Fighting through these toils and snares
Makes life very difficult and totally unclear.
It can really cloud your view,
Making it hard for you to remember
When things really did run smooth.

So why worry!
There is nothing you can do
But pray to the Lord
And know that your prayers will always get through.

I'M SEARCHING FOR YOU, LORD

I'm searching for you, Lord,
Each and ev-er-y day.
I'm slipping and falling along the way.

I pick myself up
And continue to look,
For I know you are all around me
And not just in the Holy Book.

My faith is not strong.
I keep losing my way.
Clouds come and clouds go
And sometimes they stay.

I look and I listen
But I cannot hear,
Not even a simple message from you, Lord,
To let me know that you are near.

Time after time
I am covered by thick clouds of gray
And those are the times
I must continue to pray.

I know I should not lose my faith
But I am so weak,
For when life's problems rear their heads,
I am blinded from the path that I seek.

You sent to me, my Lord,
A true witness and believer
Who is always there to show me
Your love, and how I can become a receiver.

So please be patient with me, O Lord,
And take me by the hand,
For I know your love is pure
And forever will stand.

THE CROSS

Jesus, when you were brought to the cross
And pierced through the side,
I think, oh, how you lived and oh, how you died
To give us life, yesterday, today
And in the nearby and by.

You took the twelve
And showed them oh, so many things.
How the flowers bloom
And the birds do sing,
How the blind can see,
How the dead do rise,
How the lame can walk,
And oh, how you made the mute to talk.

You said, for only believe, have faith in me,
For my Heavenly Father sent me here
To serve his people from shore to shore,
And sea to sea.

Listen with your ears and feel with your hearts
Also see with your eyes,
For I was sent to share with you,
To comfort and to love you
Before I rise.

I give all that I have,
So you may learn to live
The life my Father offers you,
For He sent me here,
Not to take but to give.

Hold fast to my word
For the time will surely come
When I am no longer with you,
For my time on earth will soon be done.

I will come back
For those who truly believe
To take you home to a life
That you truly deserve and will receive.

Come to us, Father, today and always.
Teach us to live and teach us to pray
Stay by our side, for we are weak.
Always be here with us as we continue to seek.

To seek your face,
To seek your grace,
In such a lowly and confusing place.

Oh, when I look at the cross
That they nailed you to,
I think of how and what
You have brought your people through.

THE LIGHT OF THIS WORLD

What was this light, that appeared in the skies?
Was this the brightest light
They would see tonight?
Was this the light they would see
From this point on to eternity?
Was this the light that would see them through
The world's many problems and conflicts, too?

NO! This was the Star of David
That would show them the way
To where our Newborn King would lay.

To show the wise men
Who would travel so far.
Bearing gifts for the King
In such beautiful boxes and fragrant jars.

To make them wiser even still
As not to return to Herod,
The king of ill will.

To guide the sheep and shepherds in the field
and gave them warm light to rest under,
So peaceful and still.

They were led to Jesus,
The light of THIS world.
This light would not disappear
As night turned to day,
For JESUS IS the TRUE LIGHT
To lead and guide them all the way.

Who of the wise men or shepherds in the field
Would have ever imagined
Our Savior would be born on a night
When the inn would be filled?

So may you all be blessed on this Christmas morn
And may your life's endeavors be full of hope and love,
For is not this the reason
Why our Savior was born?

So bring all your sorrows, your cares, and your woes,
And lay them at the Savior's feet.
Jesus will bear them
And he will give you much joy, happiness, and such great peace.

So shout Hallelujah and Glory to God
For Jesus the Son
Because all our sorrows and burdens
Have been fought for and already won.

Whether HE is here today
Physically or not,
HE IS LORD,
And HIS light burns FOREVER HOT!

LITTLE ANGELS

I went to the store to buy something for me.
Instead I saw a Christmas tree
Filled with names of little angels
All staring at me.

I did not know the little angels
That hung on the tree,
But I knew in my heart
What that tree meant to me.

I thought to myself,
How sad it might be
To wake up and find
Nothing under the tree.

These angels were of all ages, colors, shapes, and sizes,
Asking for different things.
I thought what happiness
One of these little gifts might bring.

If everyone would take just one little angel
And go to the store,
This act would give to so many more.

For Jesus might say something similar to,
As you do for this little one,
You do unto me.
I see ALL!
And you will be truly blessed indeed.

BLESSINGS

My pastor would be in the pulpit
Ev-er-y Sunday morn,
Preaching the word of God to the congregation,
Whether healed or torn.

He would always say,
You can receive a blessing,
Whether big or small.
I would think to myself,
What is the meaning to it all?

I would go to church Sunday after Sunday,
Waiting for a blessing to fall at my feet,
Not realizing that it could come from the words
That he continued to preach.

One morning I received a message from the word
And realized, YES, this is it.
The words felt good and truly fit.

The message touches your heart
And makes you smile,
Knowing that the Lord's word
Will prevail over any trial.

It felt so good to finally know
That the blessings my pastor spoke about
Did not have to fall from the skies
Like a thunderous shout.

No matter if the pastor reaches
Just one with the word,
It is still a job, that is well done,
For a single sinner's soul
Could have truly been won.

The blessings do come,
Whether big or small.
You have to be watching and listening
Whether they are for one or for all.

TO BE INSPIRED

How can one attempt to write?
Without being inspired!
This gift allows the mind to think
And to never tire.

The Lord spoke to me
And said you will write.
But I did not know, how or when,
Or what to write.

I would often hear people speak
Of how others had inspired them,
Not fully understanding it.
I was not privy to this knowledge
Until the Lord saw fit.

And now I know
It is when someone accepts you.
Has faith in you, and believes in you.
And all the things you might want to do.

To stand by you,
To encourage you,
To applaud and give praise,
When and wherever it is due.

To be there for you,
When no one else is around.
To lift you up,
When your spirits are down.

They give all that they have from within
To try and keep you afloat from all harm and sin.
To strengthen your mind,
So that you can see
All that is good,
And to help set your mind and your spirit free.

Giving you the will to go on.
When you feel your life
Has been embattled, scarred, and torn.

It began early one Thanksgiving morn.
As I tossed and turned
And then my thoughts were born.

I got up and picked up my pen.
That is when I learned
All my thoughts were locked within.

I wrote one verse and tried to stop!
The Lord said, "NO."
For this is one message
That will reach the top.

So I wrote on and on
And found it was so easy to do.
I did not stop!
Until my poem was finished and thoroughly reviewed.

I could go on and on
About what inspiration now means to me.
I hope this short poem
Has helped open your eyes,
And maybe you will agree.

A MESSAGE FOR MY SISTER
FROM HEART TO HEART

I often say, "O Lord, hear me pray."
He will always say, do not stray.

Come to me. I will comfort your heart.
For remember your sister will do her part.

There are days when I am so terribly low.
I look for her smile, but see a glow.

She has been there for me, no matter what.
With a cheerful word and Scripture
That always means so much.

At times she is my ears,
For I cannot hear
Your spoken words, O Lord,
Which are not always so clear.

My God, my God, so keep her near
Because your children truly need her
RIGHT HERE.

She was sent to me by my God above.
To praise Him, to thank Him,
And to give Him her love.

So, Dear Lord, please keep her safe
And in your tender care,
For she is so close and very dear.

MY CHILD'S LIFE IS DESTINED TO BE

When you were first born
And placed in my arms,
Mommy felt the Lord
Had sprinkled you with special charms.

I looked into those big beautiful eyes
And realized THEY ARE
As bright and beautiful as the stars in the skies.

You attract those around you like a magnet.
They who know you will not regret
But will always remember and never forget.

Your time will come and your light will shine.
Thank God for those who support and love you.
They will be First, and not last on your mind.

Time shall pass slowly at first,
Then you appear as a brilliant burst.

I see great things for my child so dear,
So never give up,
For your dreams are quite near.

There will be days when you stumble and fall,
But in the end, YOU SHALL achieve them all.

ERLINE DENNIS

I CHOSE YOU

I chose you, Pat, without a doubt.
To be my child's Godmommy,
With the Lord's blessings,
And the angels joyful shout.

I watched how you treated her
With a love so true.
I knew in my heart
It just had to be you.

This was the first time you met her,
She was treated like your own
With the tender care and patience
That she was shown.

You took her by the hand
As you walked down the street.
I could not keep up with the speed of your feet.

So take my child and watch her grow,
For I know you will teach her and show her
The right way to go.

Each day I thank God
Not only for you,
But also for the love that the Younger and Outlaw
families have given her, too.

You not only opened your arms and opened your hearts,
But you also opened your homes
And invited my child in
To become a part.

So hang on in there when the going gets rough,
She will make you proud one day
While strutting her stuff.

Thank God, thank God
For people like you.
My child has truly been blessed
With a Godmommy so loving and true.

FOR ALL THE YEARS YOU'VE MISSED

This is a poem to go with the book
Of all those pictures
That my Mommy took.

Of when I first came into this world
And how I became Mommy and Daddy's precious little pearl.
How I went home to live in a house.
Where I was not always as quiet as a mouse.

As the weeks and months passed by,
My Mommy would watch
With such joy and pride,
Stemming from deep, deep down inside.

They would watch me tumble and fall,
Knowing that with time,
I would stand, straight, strong, and tall.

I really did learn to talk
Before I could even stand or walk,
And I have not missed a beat
From the time I learned how to speak.

People would always ask my Mom.
When will she ever grow into those eyes!
Because my face was small
In comparison to size.

I stayed with my Grandmommy
From the time I was two months old.
She taught me how to do many things,
Like cooking and sewing,
Which are lessons worth far more
Than silver or gold.

My Grandma would call me,
Sweet Honey Dripper.
Grandmommy has since gone away
To sing and shout with the angels
All night and all day.

As you look at the pictures,
Time seems to fly by.
You can see that smile,
And sometimes a devilish gleam in my eyes.

Just look at the different expressions
That appear on my face,
Letting you know I was very happy.
Whether dressed in pants, or in ribbon and lace.

I've been to Disney World.
I went to a Philadelphia park zoo.
I've been in a beauty pageant in New York.
And now I go to dancing and acting school.

I've traveled with my Mom
To places that were new.
I've seen and done a lot of things
That most children will never be able to do.

I have grown from that little girl
With the big bright eyes
To know that my dreams can become a reality
If not today in the nearby and by.

Time has marched on.
And the Lord has sent me You.
I wanted to share all those missing years
With my Godmommy
Because you know
I love you too.

WHY MAMA?

Oh, my Lord, why did my Mama have to go?
We were blessed with her righteousness,
And her tenderness.
Now there's a great void, and much emptiness.
She is so deeply and truly missed.
And the hurt does show.
For all our hearts are broken so.

Even though we did not need to speak to Mama,
It was just knowing that she was there.
Now when we go into her kitchen,
There is only
Her empty chair.

I still cannot understand
Why to this day
Mama did not stay with us,
For we all prayed and prayed.

Lord, I thought you were supposed to hear
Your children when they pray,
With an open heart and listening ear
For every single word they say.

But this was not the case
When you took my Mom,
For now, there is always a raging storm
And very little, if ever any calm.

I need to understand the reason why
My Mama felt the need
To say good-bye.
I know she wanted to be with her Lord above,
Because throughout her life
He was always her first love.

Maybe I should be asking YOU, MAMA!
WHY, MAMA did you have to go?
Didn't you know we would miss you so!
Didn't you know it would break our hearts?
And how our lives would fall apart!

Didn't you care how we would feel?
Not being able to accept the Lord's will!
Didn't you know that some of us
Still cannot accept this?
When the loss we feel
Was so unexpected!

How could you leave us here alone?
To walk this earth's paths unknown.
I cannot believe that you did not care,
Leaving us here in such despair.
I have to ask all these questions,
Because my heart and mind
Need peace and some direction.

PART OF THE ANSWER

Lord, I asked,
Why did you take my Mom so needed?
He answered, because her work on earth was now completed.
Your Mom was a good and faithful servant,
So I called her home to be with me,
For it is YOU, now that I seek,
To draw closer to Thee.

Do not worry about your Mom,
For her life is now perfect,
And ever so calm.
She lives in glory and in splendidness
Where there is always much love and such tenderness.

I want you to always love your Lord,
For I will open many a brand new door
And do not feel so sad
With such grave sorrows,
For I will show you many brighter tomorrows.

So lift your head and lift up your eyes
To see my everlasting light.
I will be here to guide you,
Both by day and by night.

Come follow me,
For I will surely set you free.
I want you here too,
Alongside of me.

OUTSTRETCHED ARMS

Your outstretched arms
Say come to Me,
For You are all My children.
I know Your wants,
And Your ev-e-ry need.
My love for You will always be,
Permanent, steadfast, and totally free.

Jesus, I see You with Your outstretched hands,
I know just waiting to bless this land,
To bless Your people with Your Holy words,
For I know the message will be heard.

O Lord, I know
That You see by day and by night.
Not ever letting **even one**
Out of Your sight.

I know You have come
Never to leave us alone,
For we would get lost,
And can not find our way home.

Tell us what it is that You want,
For the devil does always linger
And tries to taunt

To take away the joy You give
And discourage us
From the right way to live.

To make us stray away from Thee,
And causing so much pain and misery.
To stop the devil in his tracks,
We must always remember to look ahead
And never to turn back.

Back to the life that we once lived,
Not knowing how to love,
Or how to give.

So, Lord, please keep reaching out to us,
So we can live in joy and peace
And not with anger and distrust.

THE CLOUD IN THE SKY

One day I saw THE cloud in the sky.
I thought to myself,
Oh, what a beautiful sight
With the sun's rays,
And golden beams of light.

It was a solitary gray and white cloud
In the skies so blue.
It billowed like a pillow,
With colors of ev-e-ry hue.

It stood out so pretty
With the rays of light
Jutting out from that heavenly city
Where God dwells with His angels
In splendor and perfect delight.

I thought again,
And said to myself,
This is how the Lord Jesus will arrive,
Like a cloud in the sky,
To take those home
Who have survived.

I continued to watch THE cloud as I drove,
Thinking only how beautiful
The sun shone
With ev-e-ry color of the rainbow.

ERLINE DENNIS

I know that the rays
Would be the Lord's light,
Whether he arrived by day or arrived by night.

His arms would be open
Ever so wide,
Saying come home with Me,
For I have prepared a place for you
Right by My side.

I am still impressed by THE cloud I saw,
Thinking once the cloud rolled by.
Heaven might open
Its golden doors,
Leading us to the Throne of Grace,
Knowing that we will now see
His precious face.

WHEN GOD SPEAKS

Father, because You spoke to my mind,
And said think,
I can only swim and never sink.

You touched my heart
And said, feel.
There is nothing I could do
But obey Your will.

You held my hand
And said write.
This is what I will continue to do.
As long as you keep me in sight.

If You spoke to my mind, touched my heart,
And held my hand,
There is no way my words
Cannot be heard
Throughout this land.

For who cannot obey You
When You speak?
The Holy Spirit makes you strong
And cripples defeat.

Lord, I know You answer prayers,
For one could search for many a year.
You know when the answer comes,
Because it becomes peaceful inside.
And the load you are carrying becomes lighter.
As the days go by.

This is just the beginning
Of the great things You have in store,
So please make me ready
To pass through those open doors.

PEACE OF MIND

When You gave me a peace of mind,
I could look ahead and also look behind.
I looked for wisdom and I looked for strength
As I carried on the day's chores at great length.

I thank You for the state I was in,
For You have allowed me to lift my pen.
I never thought that I could write,
But You made it possible
And blessed me with determination and much insight.

The peace and quiet that You gave,
Allowed my mind to think and save
All the thoughts that I possess
And allowed my pen to do the rest.

To let me write about things I know,
My thoughts poured out with a steady flow...
To tell a story You know best
And then my hand was allowed to rest.

Allowed to rest for a short while,
Until my mind opened up
And sent forth a brand new file.
Full of love and full of grace
To praise My Lord in that Heavenly place.

O Lord, please don't take this gift from me,
For I will be lost again in that raging sea.
But for now, my peace of mind comes and goes
And my thoughts are scattered to and fro.

Please help to restore that peace I found,
So I can remain on solid ground
To always be able to look towards
All, my tomorrows and Your Heavenly rewards.

A GRANDMA'S FACE

As I sat and watched a Grandma's face,
I knew that nothing could ever take the place
Of the tears of joy and pride,
As she watched her grandchildren dance to music
And moved ever so gracefully by.

She watched so intently
As if no one else were there.
Oh, if you could have only seen
That great big smile
That shows she really cares.

As they moved and grooved
In front of her face,
She had the brightest gleam,
That actually lit up the place.

I love to watch people's expressions.
I know this Grandma oh, so well.
If only you could have seen the joy,
That really no words can tell.

She gives great big hugs
And great big kisses
To let them know she is so proud.
For her grandchildren really do
Stand out in the crowd.

ERLINE DENNIS

If only I could recreate
The moment that I saw,
It would become the best-selling movie
In any video store.

Oh, how she loves her grandchildren so,
No matter what they do.
She always has a kind word for them,
To encourage them,
And that will always see them through.

To have a Grandma's love so tender
Is one of life's greatest splendors.
You should give your love to a child,
Because each is a baby
For only a short while.

There is a special bond between
A Grandma and her grandchildren
That nothing else can compare.
Seeing all the love, joy, and happiness
That really is truly there.

So, Grandma, keep on loving your grandchildren
As they joyfully grow.
For they will always remember that love so bold,
Which was showered on them
And will never ever grow old.

WHEN I LOOK BACK

Marlene, when I look back on the friendship we had,
It truly breaks my heart
And makes me feel extremely sad.

It's hard to believe that it can no longer be
Because of your reasons
And I hope not because of me.

I know the Lord spoke to me,
Saying, "Go to your niece,
Be there to help her and to guide her for Me.

Give her your time, your wisdom, and your love.
Let her know who sent you,
Your Heavenly Father from above.

Walk with her, talk with her.
ALWAYS, ALWAYS let her know that you are there,
For there will be many times she will despair."

I tried my best to do the Lord's will.
I guess my best was not good enough
Because our friendship is still.

AS BEST I CAN

Let me explain as best I can.
The Lord blessed Pat's and my friendship with His own hands.

This is not a friendship man-made.
Some of those may last a lifetime
Or maybe just a decade.

Our spirits are bound by a band of gold,
For only our Lord's eyes to behold.

There's nothing in this world
That could have ever hindered
This friendship the Lord has so truly rendered.

I hope these few lines have explained
Why I know this friendship was so truly ordained.

So, Marlene maybe someday you will be as truly blessed
With a friend who will do her very best.

She will help open your eyes and touch your heart.
And please, thank God for sending her to you
To treasure forever and never to part.

CHAN THE MAN

There is a little boy I know,
We call him, Chan the Man.
He is only going to be four years' old
And his real name IS,
QU'AMERE CHAN.

He has the biggest eyes
And the roundest cheeks
And most of the time
It is candy he seeks.

He looks at you with that devilish smile
While his hands are always busy,
For he is a child.

Most of the time when he can't have his way,
He stretches out on the floor
And refuses to play.

He will lie on the floor
And then go to sleep
For hours and hours
Without making a peep.

At times he will be listening to music,
And start to groove.
You will wonder to yourself,
Who taught this little boy?
To be so smooth.

He loves his Aunt Debbie,
With all his heart,
For he knows he can have his way
Because the Man is smart.

He'll often say, "I want to go to Aunt Debbie."
He'll run and he'll play
Until he becomes tired
And is made to sit down and behave.

Only Time will tell
And we shall see
What the future has in store
For the Man to achieve.

A DEAR FRIEND OF MINE,
TRULY YOU KNOW

I've known this lady a long, long time.
She was once a teacher of mine.

There was always something about her I admired,
But in class we would fight
Because we were both strong-willed and never tired.

She was always so strong
And very tough,
But very confident, because she knew her stuff.

We would go round for round, and surely I knew
I would be sent to the office, for being so rude.

The next day would come,
She would take me back,
Knowing to prepare for another attack.

Even though I was a pain in class that day,
And tried to alarm her,
She would always call me, "The little charmer."

I was having much fun,
As kids often do.
While she was trying to make me abide
By her class rules.

After school I would go to her room,
For I knew she would be there.
We would talk for hours and hours.
Because I knew she really cared.

Sometimes we meet people along the way,
And God gave me the wisdom to know
That she was in my life to stay.

As the years pass by,
We still keep in touch,
For in her heart she knows
I miss her so very much.

MY FRIEND THROUGHOUT THE YEARS

Pauline, you have always been so thoughtful and kind.
You will always occupy a place in my mind.

I truly thank you for the things that you do.
If only there were more people like you,
Believe me,
The world's problems would be so few.

I cannot buy you gifts to show gratitude.
I can only speak and write words
That will never elude.

Continue to be and always stay
As thoughtful and giving
As you are today.

Thank you for being my friend
And always willing to extend.
Thank you for being there
And for all the good times
We were blessed to share.

Others may not know you, as I do,
But I know the Lord will bless you too.

So never give up hope,
As we sometimes do.
For always know the Lord
Will see you through.

ERLINE DENNIS

THE GYPSY IN ME

There is a gypsy that abides in me.
She will visit me occa-sion-ally.
That gypsy in me has been resting for a while,
But I KNOW that this is just not her style.

This gypsy in me is due to appear
And when she does,
I must watch for her
And be prepared.

Let's get in the wind
And have some fun,
For there is no doubt in my mind
I am ready to run.

This gypsy will beckon,
Come go with me
And please hold on tight,
For as you know, I am in control
Of this wondrous and glorious flight.

There are times when she beckons and calls,
Come right now and have a ball.
But what she fails to realize
Is that the cash is low,
So I have to bow my head,
And sometimes forego.

The spring is here
And I feel fancy free,
For I am on
An "I want to do" spree.

I want to do this
And I want to do that
As long as I have someone to run with,
You might as well say
The plans are a wrap.

When the gypsy in me
Becomes stifled and hindered,
She becomes angry and bitter
And not easy to render.

She has her seasons to appear,
But when she is asleep,
It is as if she never cared.

SUCH A SAD LITTLE FACE

When I look at that sad little face,
I wish I could be with you always
To help you run this race.

And to see all the hurt and sadness there,
My heart breaks for you
And makes me know
That you need all my love
And tender care.

You have not even begun to live.
Yet my poor child feels so much sadness,
With so much love inside to give,
I want to walk every mile of this road with you.
But I know that this is something
I cannot do.

Don't let others get you down,
Always show off that pretty smile
And never, ever,
Let them see you frown.

Hold your head up high.
My child,
And wipe away all those tears,
For happiness is yours to have
And to enjoy for many a year.

So let the light shine in those beautiful eyes
And don't ever let anyone make you cry.
Your life should be full of joy and pleasure.
That not even time or space can measure.

Let them know
You are proud of WHO and WHAT you are,
For you will become a bright and shining star.

Take heed to my words
And have no fear,
For your future is written on High.
And in the hands of ONE
Who knows all and truly cares.

The best that I can do
Is to always encourage you
to support and pray for you
When your days are so lonely
And terribly blue.

Always keep close to your heart
What you believe,
And no one can ever take away
What is rightfully yours to receive.

ERLINE DENNIS

TO SEVER THE TIES

I do not want to make any more friends.
They seem to always leave in the end.
You trust them with words from the heart.
You share good times and bad times,
But somehow they see fit to depart.

Life has too many ups and downs,
Causing many a smile
To turn into frowns.
Life is so unfair at times,
Leaving us many a mountain to climb.

I hold on much too tight.
When others let go.
I must learn to sever the ties
And ask the Lord
To please lessen the blow.

Holding on causes too much grief
Because it can sour
A person's religious beliefs.
The sorrow becomes too much to bear
And in time, teaches you not to care.

Why must life have so many toils and troubles?
Bursting many a precious bubble,
Causing us to walk away
From all life may have to offer
From day to day.

What becomes of the joy
That gets washed down the drain
When life showers us
With so much sorrow and pain!

Not wanting to face another sorrow,
We must look to and give thanks to God,
For only God knows
What belongs to tomorrow.

ERLINE DENNIS

I MUST WALK BY FAITH, NOT BY SIGHT

If you could know what I know
And feel what I feel,
You would understand
That this IS the Lord's will.

I have to walk by faith
And not by sight.
Believe in the Lord
And all HIS might.

To walk by faith
And not by sight
Is a true test of one's beliefs?
That all things will turn out right.

If I go into this negatively
With doubt in my mind
And doubt in my heart,
I am defeated
Before I ever start.

Just like Peter
On the wide open sea,
Jesus said, "Come, Peter.
Come to me."

Peter started to walk by faith.
Then he began to doubt.
He started to sink
And all he could do was shout.

Sometimes we must venture into the unknown,
And know that the Lord is watching,
From His Almighty throne.

WHEN HE KNOCKS AT THE DOOR

I once saw a picture, of Our Lord.
HE was standing and knocking, outside a door.
The door had no knob to let HIM in,
For HE will continue to knock, from now until then.

When the Lord knocks at the door,
You are the only one
Who can let HIM in,
For there is no knob for HIM to turn
To allow the Lord entrance
To cleanse away all your sins.

When your heart and your mind
Are ready to accept HIS love,
He will shower you with
HIS grace and HIS peace from Heaven above.

Give your life to HIM.
So HE can renew your spirit and renew your soul
And make you brand new
To sparkle and shine like pure gold.

HE knows everything about you
Whether hidden or in sight.
The Lord can make you as different
As day is to night.

So trust in the Lord
With all your heart.
We are all his children.
HE promises to be with us always
And HE will never depart.

WE'LL ALWAYS REMEMBER – 9/11

This is a tribute to 9/11,
When so many innocent souls have entered heaven.
So many families have suffered so much.
But not only us, our friends from around the world have also been so
    deeply touched.

I heard of this pace where there is no more pain and no more sorrow,
Where your loved ones are graced by God's love and endless tomorrows.
It takes a lot to rebuild what terrorism has left behind,
But the pain and sorrow can only be healed,
By God, the true and divine.

We have made great strides since that fated day,
The rubble has been cleared up as the pace picked up along the way.
Many hearts will remain broken for some time to come,
But with faith, hope, and prayer,
These 3 will be comforting to some.

To all those who have strived through the toil,
Never forgetting our men and women on foreign soil.
We salute and praise you for your remarkable skills,
And for your strength, bravery and unwavering will.

God's blessings to those who worked long, hard, and endless hours,
To search for and rescue, the victims from the fallen Twin Towers.

Our hats off to our men and women who are fighting the war.
To keep our nation safe and terrorism away from our American shores.
Never relentless in the fight,
To keep our great red, white and blue forever flying freely by day and by night.

Again, thanks to you all,
You will be remembered in our prayers.
For if not for you and your efforts,
We would continue to struggle and live in constant fear.

TO OUR FIGHTING MEN AND WOMEN

God bless you all,
For defending our nation.
I pray that the Lord watch over each and every one of you,
During this war's duration.

We at home are so proud of you.
As you defend our flag,
The great red, white and blue.

I wish you all strength, courage and love,
As I know our Lord sends His light,
To shine on you from heaven above.

I wish you a Merry Christmas.
And a Happy New Year.
For we have seen so many broken hearts.
And people all over the world
Have shed rivers of tears.

Again I say, God bless you all,
Because we know.
You will not let our great nation fall.

WITH A MOTHER'S HANDS

If I could I would reach inside,
Not with a surgeon's hands,
But with the gentle touch,
Of a mother's hands.

To mend that broken little heart,
That seems so strained and torn apart.
To patch that broken little soul,
With all the tender love a mother knows.

To help lift that downcast spirit,
To heights unknown,
To help turn your live around.
With joy, hope, peace and love,
That will never let you down.

To brighten up your days,
That are so bleak and very gray.
To help you see your way through,
And accept all the blessings,
That the Lord has in store for you.

To mend those broken little wings,
To give your heart a new song - to forever sing
To make those bright eyes smile again,
For happiness is yours to seek and win.

Talk to me – you can lean on me.
For you are the only one who can see.
Tell me what is wrong,
For I will stand tall for you and be very strong.

Please help me to understand,
The pain that is so obvious to see.
For it is written all over your little face,
Where no joy or laugh lines can be traced.

Look to the Lord,
For His plan is such,
That not even the weary,
Will suffer for much.

ERLINE DENNIS

A BLESSING TO BEHOLD

This was an awesome labor of love.
Not only all around us, but also from up above
To see so many people pull together as one,
Was truly a mighty victory we have all shared and won.

To build a house for a family we do not even know.
This is one of the greatest compassions man could ever show.

So many, many people from all walks of life,
Have come together for this family,
Who have been through several misfortunes and strife.
So many different talents and remarkable skills,
Have all come together for the same goal and good will.

As I watched for hour upon hour,
All the hearts and hands working together with love and The
    Almighty's power.
I also wanted to lend a helping hand,
So I donned my hard hat and took a stand.

My heart was touched and I was inspired to write this poem,
Wishing you and your family, peace, joy and happiness in your
    elegant new home.
This truly was a blessing to behold,
As I know memories shared in your new surroundings,
Will become more precious to you than silver or gold.

SONGS TO CREATE – MEMORIES TO SHARE

To my niece Miranda on your special day,
Which I thought would be much, much further away.
In our family there are very few occasions like this,
This is one of those days we would never miss.

We wish you luck, peace and joy.
And we wish you love.
But the most important, agape, the unconditional love,
From your Heavenly Father who sits above.

When the troubles do come,
With the rain and the thunder.
Always remember the vows you make here today,
"What God has joined together, let no man put asunder".

As you two walk this road of life,
Which will have many surprises.
Remember you will have to share,
And to make many, many compromises.

There will be days with the most precious tomorrows,
That will wash away the yesterdays of many sorrows.

Hold tight to each other's hands as you go along,
For you will create your own special and original songs.
Songs and memories to last while you mature and grow old,
To share with family and friends,
From your treasure chest as memories unfold.

GOLDEN WINGS

Dedicated to the Families and the Newtown Community

What words can be spoken,
When so many, many, many hearts have been broken.
So much pain and so many tears shed by nations,
Because the lives of the innocent were suddenly taken.

We wrap our arms around you with blankets of love,
As we pray and seek guidance from heaven above.
Hold their memories close to your heart,
These memories will keep you close,
And never far apart.

I cannot even imagine the pain and sorrow parents feel,
Or how long it will take for broken hearts to heal.
Rest assure your precious angels are in a safer place,
Where they know no more pain or sorrows.
Because NOW they are blest with forever tomorrows.

God sees your tears and feels your pain,
For He carries your loved ones in His arms once again.
Our Father truly loves them so,
He will wrap them in His arms and never ever let go.

Peace and love only abide there,
Where there are no such things as pain or fear.
They are now angels with golden wings,
Captured in heaven's glory.
While the angels praise His name and forever sing.

ABOUT THE AUTHOR

Erline is the 10th child of 11 children. Ms. Dennis was born and raised in Connecticut and is a graduate of the University of Bridgeport. She has one daughter, Shante'. Erline began writing at the age of 42 early on Thanksgiving morning in 1995. She did not choose to write, she was chosen. The Lord spoke to her heart, she listened and followed the Lord's lead. Ms. Dennis never liked to write, never thought about writing and never wanted to write. She wrote her 1st poem, *A Message for My Sister from Heart to Heart*, to her dear friend and sister Patricia.

Printed in the United States
by Baker & Taylor Publisher Services